THE 10™

Best Animal Helpers

Melissa Carnelos

Series Editor
Jeffrey D. Wilhelm

Much thought, debate, and research went into choosing and ranking the 10 items in each book in this series. We realize that everyone has his or her own opinion of what is most significant, revolutionary, amazing, deadly, and so on. As you read, you may agree with our choices, or you may be surprised — and that's the way it should be!

Franklin Watts®

an imprint of

◪SCHOLASTIC

www.scholastic.com/librarypublishing

A Rubicon book published in association with Scholastic Inc.

Rubicon © 2008 Rubicon Publishing Inc.

Associate Publishers: Kim Koh, Miriam Bardswich
Project Editor: Amy Land
Editor: Mariana Aldave
Creative Director: Jennifer Drew
Project Manager/Designer: Jeanette MacLean
Senior Graphic Designer: Gabriela Castillo
Graphic Designer: Rebecca Buchanan

The publisher gratefully acknowledges the following for permission to reprint copyrighted material in this book.

Every reasonable effort has been made to trace the owners of copyrighted material and to make due acknowledgment. Any errors or omissions drawn to our attention will be gladly rectified in future editions.

"Bee Buzz Scares off African Elephants" (excerpt) by Susan Brown for National Geographic News, October 9, 2007. Permission courtesy of National Geographic Image Collection.

"Death Comes Purring" (excerpt from "At Rhode Island nursing home, death comes purring"). From CBC News, July 26, 2007. Used with permission of the Associated Press © 2006 All Rights Reserved.

Cover image: Woman and black Labrador retriever, helping to search the World Trade Center rubble following the September 11, 2001 attacks– AP Photo/Alan Diaz

Library and Archives Canada Cataloguing in Publication

Carnelos, Melissa
      The 10 best animal helpers / Melissa Carnelos.

Includes index.
ISBN: 978-1-55448-516-1

      1. Readers (Elementary). 2. Readers—Animal helpers.
I. Title. II. Title: Ten best animal helpers.

PE1117.C365 2007   428.6   C2007-906914-2

1 2 3 4 5 6 7 8 9 10   10   17 16 15 14 13 12 11 10 09 08

Printed in Singapore   32222000178063

Contents

LEAN
ON
ME

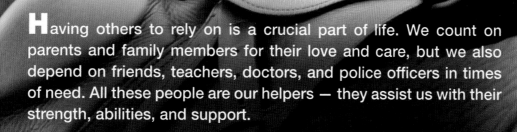

Having others to rely on is a crucial part of life. We count on parents and family members for their love and care, but we also depend on friends, teachers, doctors, and police officers in times of need. All these people are our helpers — they assist us with their strength, abilities, and support.

Humans have animal helpers, too. Some animals provide emotional or physical comfort. Others protect us in times of danger or heal our wounds when we get hurt. Still others work alongside us, performing extraordinary physical feats to assist us.

In this book, we focus on 10 animals that have made a difference in our lives. We ranked these animal helpers by asking ourselves the following questions: How smart is the animal? How sociable is it? How supportive is it of people in need? How does it work alongside people? And finally, how closely does it live and associate with humans? Keep these questions in mind and as you read, ask yourself …

sociable: *likely to seek or enjoy companionship*

WHAT IS OUR BEST ANIMAL HELPER?

(10) LEECHES

Getting bitten by a leech is not as painful as you may think!

CLASSIFICATION AND SIZE: Leeches are segmented worms. On average, leeches measure between one inch and eight inches long. The largest leeches can be 18 inches long.

HOW THEY HELP: Doctors can use the leech's bloodsucking appetites for medical purposes.

Bloodsucking leeches latch onto and feed on fish, frogs, turtles, and even humans. As scary as this might sound, leeches are not all bad! In fact, their name comes from the Anglo-Saxon word *loece*, which means "to heal."

Though they might not look very friendly, leeches have helped humans for thousands of years. In medieval times, people used to turn to leeches as a natural cure for all sorts of aches and pains. Today, doctors increasingly accept leeches as a reliable form of treatment for surgery patients. Turn the page to find out why you should not be afraid of this bloodsucker's bite ...

LEECHES

PROFILE

Some leeches live off the blood and tissue of other animals for nourishment. Others feed on algae or on microorganisms living on another animal's body. Leeches are hermaphrodites (her-mah-fro-dites) — they have both male and female reproductive organs. They can flatten their bodies, curl into a ball, or go completely limp to evade predators. As they feed, bloodsucking leeches will secrete an anticoagulant to thin the host's blood so they can suck up the blood more easily.

COUNT ON ME

Leeches are being used today in plastic and reconstructive surgery. The natural anticoagulant they secrete as they feed helps to fight blood clots and restore blood flow to a surgery patient's wounds. Recently, doctors have started using leeches to treat patients with arthritic pain because leech saliva also reduces painful swelling.

anticoagulant: *substance that prevents blood from clotting*

IN THE NEWS

In 2001, researchers at the University of Wisconsin created a mechanical version of the medicinal leech. The sterile glass device has several advantages over its flesh-and-blood counterpart. It is better at delivering anticoagulants, and it can remove more blood from a larger area of tissue. "But perhaps the mechanical device's biggest advantage," said one of the inventors, "is that it is not a leech."

sterile: *free from microscopic living things, especially germs*

How would you feel about being treated with a medicinal leech? Explain.

The mechanical leech created by researchers at the University of Wisconsin

Quick Fact

The use of any living organism for medical treatments is called biotherapy. Biotherapy includes drugs, vaccines, and antitoxins that are made from living things.

COUNTING LEECHES

Check out this list of numbers for more information about leeches!

People began using leeches **2,500** years ago for everything from bloodletting to curing headaches to healing cuts.

Scientists have identified more than **600** species of leeches around the world.

The body of a leech is made up of **34** segments.

Leeches can suck **0.67** oz of blood in one sitting.

Leeches can have **2–10** simple eyes, according to their species. They cannot see images but can detect some movement and changes in the intensity of light.

The mouthparts of leeches can have **300** razor-sharp teeth.

It costs doctors about **$7–$8** to buy a medicinal leech.

Leeches usually feed for **20–30** minutes before falling off.

bloodletting: *removal of blood, usually from a vein, as a therapeutic measure*
intensity: *degree of energy or strength*

The Expert Says...

"Nature's medicines — often called 'gross' — are sometimes the best. Doctors are likely to turn to … leeches only when nothing else works."

— Michele Root-Bernstein, author of *Honey, Mud, Maggots, and Other Medical Marvels*

Take Note

Leeches crawl to spot #10 on our list! They have been helping doctors for more than 2,000 years. They can help heal or bring relief to people suffering from various medical conditions. Leeches might not look the part but they certainly are a handy helper to have around!

• Are you surprised that leeches made the list? How can an animal that feeds off the blood and tissue of other animal species be considered a helper to humans? Explain your answer.

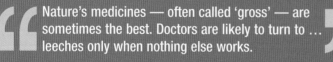

5   **4**   **3**   **2**   **1**

⑨ BATS

Some bats eat their own weight in insects each night.

BAT CHASING MOTH–MICHAEL DURHAM/ MINDEN PICTURES/GETTY IMAGES

CLASSIFICATION AND SIZE: Bats are mammals. They can be less than one inch in length or as long as 15 inches; their wingspan can be as wide as five feet.

HOW THEY HELP: Bats are natural pollinators and pest exterminators, and their saliva can be used to treat various medical conditions.

Bats are some of the most fascinating creatures in the animal kingdom. They are vastly different from all other mammals. They can fly. To save energy, they can lower their body temperature when it is cold. They also live much longer than other animal species of similar size.

Bats are also perhaps the most misunderstood animals in the world. Many people are scared of bats or think that they are very dangerous. But most bats are insectivores, which means they feed mainly on insects. Some bats eat fruit, nectar, or pollen. Carnivorous species hunt birds, rodents, reptiles, and other bats. The bats that get the most attention are the infamous vampires that suck the blood of humans and other larger mammals.

Even though bats might look strange and they might have a bad reputation, they actually do a lot of good. Find out more about their contributions before you banish bats from your list of best animal helpers.

---

infamous: *having a very bad reputation*

BATS

PROFILE

Bats are the only mammals that can fly. They are nocturnal, which means they are active only at night. Some bats detect their prey and surroundings by using echolocation. Others cannot echolocate but have highly developed eyesight. Most bats have a great sense of smell, too. Bats usually live in caves, forests, and abandoned mines and buildings. Most species of bats give birth to just one or two offspring a year.

echolocation: *method of sending out high-pitched sounds and using the echoes to locate objects*

? Many species of bats are in danger of becoming extinct because humans are destroying their natural habitats. What do you think can be done to prevent the situation from getting worse?

A bat may live about 30 years, but a mouse of a similar size would live just one year.

COUNT ON ME

Bats are of great help to farmers — they eat insects that would damage crops, and their droppings are useful natural fertilizers. Bats are also pollinators and seed dispersers. Without bats, we would not have bananas, mangoes, cashews, or hundreds of other fruits and nuts. Recently, doctors began to use the saliva of certain bats to treat stroke patients. Bat spit has a powerful substance that can help prevent blood clots.

IN THE NEWS

In 2006, researchers reported that pest-eating bats help corn, cotton, and other crop farmers in parts of Texas save close to $1.7 million a year. This amount covers the costs of pesticides and the damage prey would do to crops. Although researchers focused their study on eight counties in Texas, they said that bats benefit farmers in the Midwest and Canada, too.

? As natural pest exterminators, bats not only help farmers, but they also benefit the natural environment. How do you think that is?

These fruit bats help the distribution of plants by scattering the seeds of the fruit they eat.

The Expert Says...

" Bats are keystone species in our ecosystem. They play a vital role in maintaining it, and if disturbed or reduced, the ecosystem as we know it will collapse. "

— Dr. Michael Gannon, Professor of Biology, Pennsylvania State University

keystone: *essential element that supports a whole*

10 9 8 7 6

BUSTING VAMPIRE BAT MYTHS

Check out this Q&A to learn more about the infamous vampire bat.

Q When do they attack?

A Vampire bats attack at night, when their victims are asleep.

Q What do they do when they attack?

A The bat first locates the veins of the animal. It then uses its sharp teeth to make a shallow cut. Because bat saliva contains a numbing substance, victims usually do not wake up during the attack. The bat simply laps up a small amount of blood and then flies away.

Q Will vampire bats attack humans?

A Vampire bats rarely attack humans. Besides, most people sleep indoors and far away from the natural habitats of vampire bats.

Q Who or what do bats feed on?

A Vampire bats feed mostly on the blood of cattle and other livestock, such as pigs and horses. They sometimes also feed on birds.

Q Why else might vampire bats have a bad reputation?

A Vampire bats can carry disease-causing viruses, such as rabies. They can transmit viruses when they bite their victims.

Quick Fact

Vampire bats are found only in Central and South America. Contrary to popular fiction, vampire bats are not found anywhere in Europe.

Take Note

The bat swoops into the #9 spot. Even though bats are often thought of as scary, bloodthirsty creatures of the night, they are actually very helpful to people. Farmers rely on them to keep pests under control. Doctors consider their saliva a lifesaver. Finally, ecosystems rely on bats as pollinators and seed dispersers.

- Why do you think people have developed scary stories and fears about the bat?

8 HONEYBEES

These bees are building a honeycomb.

CLASSIFICATION AND SIZE: Honeybees are insects. They are less than an inch long.

HOW THEY HELP: Honeybees help crops and other plants grow and reproduce; they also produce honey and beeswax.

Honeybees play a vital role in the food chain — they pollinate plants and enable them to grow and reproduce. Without honeybees, many different wild plants and important food crops would not exist. In fact, scientists believe that honeybees played a key role in the evolution of the wide variety of flowers in the world by spreading pollen among various plants.

But there's more. Honeybees produce honey and beeswax, both of which humans treasure. During the Stone Age thousands of years ago, people used to steal honey from the hives of wild bees! Another useful quality of honeybees is their great sense of smell. They can quickly tell if something has changed in their environment. Some day, buzzing bees might be able to warn humans of danger!

HONEYBEES

Bee collecting nectar

PROFILE

Honeybees have a special honey stomach in which they carry nectar. They bring the nectar back to their hives, where it is turned into honey and used as food. Honeybees also produce beeswax from their bodies. They work 24 hours a day and communicate by buzzing or by doing a dance.

COUNT ON ME

As honeybees fly around looking for food, they spread pollen from one flower to another. This pollinates, or fertilizes, the plants and allows them to reproduce. Many plants — from those in the wild to food crops that humans depend on — could not exist without the help of honeybees. In the past, people often used raw honey to treat aches and pains, as well as burns and cuts. Today, people eat honey as food and use beeswax to make candles, cosmetics, and other products.

IN THE NEWS

In 2007, researchers from the University of Montana found that bees could help warn us of toxic chemicals nearby. Within 30 seconds of detecting a poison in the air, bees begin to buzz much differently from normal. "The sounds bees produce can actually tell [us] what chemical is hitting them," said researcher Jerry Bromenshenk. The finding could lead to a device for soldiers that alerts them to toxic chemicals that could be used in warfare.

Quick Fact

Agriculture in North America relies on honeybees to pollinate close to 100 varieties of plants that produce fruits, vegetables, berries, and nuts.

The Expert Says...

" Not only have the products of bees been of great value to humans, the bees themselves have provided useful services. "

— May R. Berenbaum, author of *Bugs in the System*

Quick Fact

Honeybee populations around the world are declining drastically. This phenomenon is called Colony Collapse Disorder. Scientists believe the bees might be suffering from an unknown contagious disease.

10   9   **8**   7   6

BEE BUZZ SCARES OFF AFRICAN ELEPHANTS

An article from National Geographic News
By Susan Brown, October 9, 2007

Recordings of angry bees are enough to send even big, tough African elephants scrambling, a new study says. ...

Bees might someday help farmers protect their crops from being trampled by elephants.

As some elephant populations in Africa grow larger and more land is cleared for agriculture, elephants are clashing with humans. A few have even trampled farmers.

Lucy King, a zoologist with the Nairobi, Kenya-based nonprofit Save the Elephants ... is working with farmers in the Laikipia district of Kenya to develop strategies for keeping elephants away. In that area, maize, beans, and squash are among the most common crops lost to elephants. ...

King wanted to see if African honeybees might deter elephants from eating crops. ... King tracked down elephant families in Samburu National Reserve in northern Kenya. In multiple trials, she hid a wireless speaker in a fake tree trunk near each group of elephants, then drove away.

From a distance, King triggered the prerecorded sound of angry bees. ... Half the elephant groups departed within ten seconds. ...

Bees can't sting through thick adult elephant skin, but the insects do find a few vulnerable spots. They are attracted to the elephant's watery eyes and will "go up the trunk, which must be awful," King said.

Take Note

Honeybees buzz to a #8 ranking. Not only do they pollinate all sorts of plants but they also produce honey and beeswax. Many people are afraid of their stings, but honeybees normally do not sting unless they perceive their hives to be in danger. They are actually helpful insects.
• May Berenbaum also says we have "taken advantage" of honeybees for many years. Do you agree with this description of our relationship with honeybees? Explain your answer.

? Driving hungry elephants away from crops saves them from conflict with farmers. But do you think this is the best solution for these elephants? Explain.

7 PIGEONS

Many visitors to Venice, Italy, enjoy feeding the local pigeons.

CLASSIFICATION AND SIZE: Pigeons are birds. Most pigeons are between 10 and 15 inches long.

HOW THEY HELP: Pigeons can carry important messages and packages, and they can be kept as pets to provide companionship.

Throughout history, pigeons have been known to be reliable messenger birds. There are hundreds of species of pigeons living in all parts of the world. They have helped deliver lifesaving messages, medications, and even small packages. These birds can fly for many miles in all kinds of weather. Even when faced with danger, they will keep going to complete their mission.

Pigeons have much better eyesight and can find their way around much more quickly than humans. They are also extremely adaptable and can be found in jungles, woodlands, open fields, cliffs, and even city streets. They often fly in large flocks, mainly to increase the chances of getting food and to protect themselves from predators.

FEEDING PIGEONS—ISTOCKPHOTO

PIGEONS

PROFILE

Pigeons can adapt to different environments. They are territorial and do not migrate. Some pigeons can reach speeds of up to 90 miles per hour. No matter how far they fly, pigeons can always find their way back home. They can sense Earth's magnetic field thanks to magnetic-like iron particles in their beaks. Psychologists at Brown University did a study of pigeons that were able to learn all 26 letters of the English alphabet.

COUNT ON ME

Throughout history, pigeons have helped deliver important messages and even parcels of medicine — and they have done so with speed and great success. They were highly prized in times of war when other forms of communication did not work. In parts of the world, such as France and New Zealand, some people still turn to pigeons to carry messages. Today, large numbers of pigeons are kept for companionship and for racing. Some people even raise pigeons and then let them go free, but the birds fly back home on their own.

---

territorial: *inclined to claim and defend an area*
migrate: *move from one region or climate to another*

IN THE NEWS

In the 1980s, the United States Coast Guard and Navy started Project Sea Hunt. The goal was to have pigeons help find people who are lost at sea. Trainers coached the pigeons to peck a key when they spotted the bright orange color used for life jackets. Over time, the birds became adept at spotting actual vests floating in open water.

? What do you look for in a pet? Would you keep a pigeon as a pet? Why or why not?

Small white pigeons, commonly known as doves, are sometimes released during wedding ceremonies. They are a symbol of peace and love.

Quick Fact

Historians have discovered evidence that people in Egypt tamed pigeons almost 12,000 years ago.

The Expert Says...

"The UK's National Pigeon Service called up more than 500,000 birds to serve during the two world wars. So important was their contribution, ferrying vital messages to troops and secret agents alike, Hitler ordered all Britain-bound birds to be fired upon."

— Peter Bryant, chairperson, Royal Pigeon Racing Association

Roll Call

Here are the profiles of two pigeons that answered the call of duty during World Wars I and II ...

Name: Cher Ami

ACT OF BRAVERY: In October 1918, a group of American soldiers became trapped behind enemy lines. They were completely surrounded by German soldiers. Because their radios were not working, the American soldiers decided to put Cher Ami into action. The pigeon was sent to headquarters with a message for help. Along the way, Cher Ami was shot at — it lost a leg and was even blinded — but it successfully delivered the message. A rescue effort was immediately launched and the soldiers were saved.

Name: G. I. Joe

ACT OF BRAVERY: In October 1943, British troops were trying to capture a German-held village in Italy. The British asked Allied forces to provide air support — to bomb the area — before they went in. When the British managed to capture the village on their own, they had to call off the scheduled bombing. So they sent the pigeon G. I. Joe to deliver the important message. Joe made it just in time to save thousands of lives.

Messenger pigeons often wore carrying cases on their backs.

English soldiers releasing a messenger pigeon during World War II

Quick Fact

Reuters News Service is today the largest international multimedia news agency. Did you know that when Reuters was founded in the early 1850s, it used carrier pigeons to transport news across a gap in the telegraph line between Berlin, Germany, and Paris, France?

Take Note

Pigeons flock to the #7 spot on our list. These birds are reliable even in dangerous times and they never let us down. With training, they could be a great help to search-and-rescue workers. And some people keep pigeons as companions.
• Why do you think the role of the pigeon as a messenger bird has changed over time? Explain your answer.

6 ELEPHANTS

Just as human babies suck their thumbs, elephant calves often suck their trunks for comfort.

CLASSIFICATION AND SIZE: Elephants are mammals. They can be more than 12 feet tall and can weigh between 8,000 and 13,000 pounds.

HOW THEY HELP: Elephants are strong enough to help loggers and rescue workers, but they are also gentle enough to help save injured people.

These enormous mammals have larger-than-life personalities to match their giant size and strength. They are intelligent and sophisticated. They show complex emotions and have been known to cry from frustration. Elephants are social animals that live in herds. They will rush headfirst into danger to save other elephants in their herd. They will even save humans — elephants have been used to rescue humans during major natural disasters.

Elephants do not see or hear very well. But they have keen senses of smell and touch. In fact, they are extremely sensitive to ground vibrations. Scientists say this ability might explain why elephants seem to have a sixth sense for anticipating disasters such as earthquakes and tsunamis.

With such amazing features and abilities, it is too bad that elephants are only found naturally in parts of Southeast Asia and Africa. Turn the page to find out more about how great a helper the elephant is to humankind.

ELEPHANTS

PROFILE

Elephants are the largest land animals in the world. Female elephants, called cows, live in family herds with their young. Adult males, called bulls, tend to roam around on their own. Elephants spend roughly two-thirds of the day looking for food. They can eat as much as 300 pounds of vegetation a day. They sleep only four to five hours a night and cannot lie down for too long or they could crush their internal organs.

COUNT ON ME

Elephants have been put to use in many battles and wars throughout history. Today, elephants help workers in the timber industry in countries such as India and Indonesia. They can push over partly cut trees and pick up and carry heavy logs using their trunks and tusks.

IN THE NEWS

In December 2004, a massive tsunami battered the shores of Sumatra (an island of Indonesia), Sri Lanka, Thailand, and nearby areas. Rescue and cleanup workers in Indonesia quickly came to rely on the help of local elephants. The elephants worked six hours every day removing debris and recovering bodies. With their strong and agile trunks, the elephants reached into places that machinery could not. Sadly, many of the elephants were injured — nails, broken timber, and jagged metal sheets cut their trunks.

Quick Fact

Elephants use their trunks to locate food and grasp enemies, examine or pick up objects, and give themselves dust or water baths.

Elephants were used to salvage useful wood from the tsunami rubble in Uleelheule district in northern Sumatra, Indonesia.

Quick Fact

A person who trains and handles elephants is called a mahout (muh-howt). A mahout always stays with the same elephant, teaching it to obey a number of different commands.

? What do you think it takes to be a mahout? What kinds of traits or skills would be required? Explain.

The Expert Says...

" Humankind has been affected, even shaped and defined, by its millennia-long relationship with elephants ... [which has been] more influential, and in some ways closer, than humankind's relationships to dogs, horses, and cats ... . "

— Eric Scigliano, author of *Love, War, and Circuses: The Age-Old Relationship Between Elephants and Humans*

CHARGE!

In ancient times, elephants were an important weapon for many warring armies. They trampled on anything and anyone in sight! This timeline runs through the history of war elephants ...

331 B.C.: Battle of Gaugamela (Goh-guh-meh-la)

Alexander the Great of Macedonia meets Darius III of Persia. The Persian army mounts an attack with 15 elephants leading the charge. Alexander wins, but not before the war elephants succeed in frightening many of his men and horses.

326 B.C.: Battle of the Hydaspes (Hi-das-pez) River

Alexander the Great fights his fourth and last battle in Asia. He faces Porus, one of the most powerful kings in India, who has 200 elephants in his army. Alexander wins the battle and even captures 80 elephants.

280 B.C.: Battle of Heraclea (Hera-clee-a)

Pyrrhus, king of Epirus, leads an invasion of Italy with an army that includes 20 elephants. Upon seeing this line of elephants, the Roman infantry runs in fear and even the cavalry refuses to charge.

cavalry: *horse-mounted military unit*

217 B.C.: Battle of Raphia (Ra-fee-uh)

Antiochus III the Great, leader of the Seleucid Empire, and Ptolemy IV, king of Egypt, face off in an epic battle. Both lead a huge army with elephants charging on the left and right to obstruct and break up the enemy's cavalry.

Quick Fact

The invention of gunpowder, cannons, and other modern weapons brought an end to the use of elephants in war.

An illustration of a Persian war elephant in battle

? How do you feel about animals helping in war?

Take Note

The elephant stomps into the #6 spot. It instinctively protects its own kind, but it is also known to help humans in need. Its size and strength made it a vital part of armies in ancient times. Today, it continues to work alongside humans, both in the timber industry and in disaster cleanup efforts.
• How do you think researchers can develop better technologies to predict natural disasters by studying an animal like the elephant?

(5) MULES

Mules are used for transportation in Hydra, Greece, where the rocky terrain is too steep for vehicles.

MULE—© JON HICKS/CORBIS

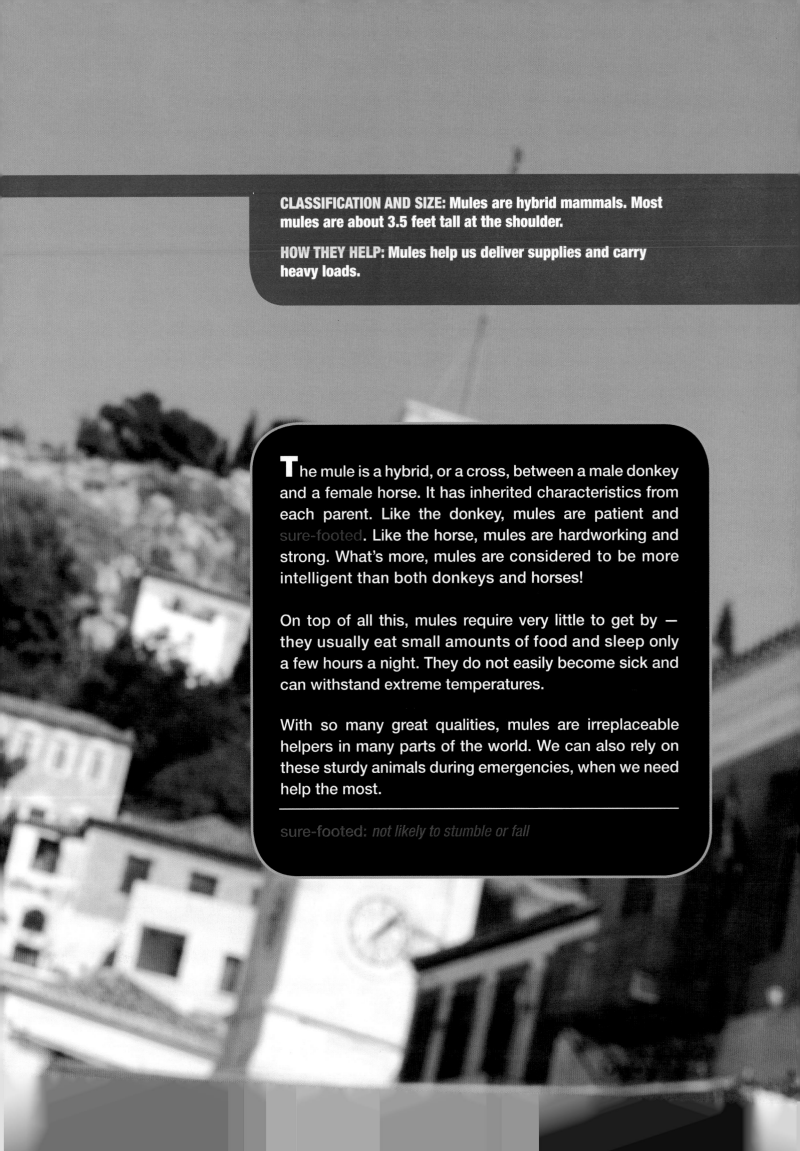

CLASSIFICATION AND SIZE: Mules are hybrid mammals. Most mules are about 3.5 feet tall at the shoulder.

HOW THEY HELP: Mules help us deliver supplies and carry heavy loads.

The mule is a hybrid, or a cross, between a male donkey and a female horse. It has inherited characteristics from each parent. Like the donkey, mules are patient and sure-footed. Like the horse, mules are hardworking and strong. What's more, mules are considered to be more intelligent than both donkeys and horses!

On top of all this, mules require very little to get by — they usually eat small amounts of food and sleep only a few hours a night. They do not easily become sick and can withstand extreme temperatures.

With so many great qualities, mules are irreplaceable helpers in many parts of the world. We can also rely on these sturdy animals during emergencies, when we need help the most.

sure-footed: *not likely to stumble or fall*

MULES

PROFILE

Like the donkey, the mule has long ears, a short mane, and small feet. Like the horse, the mule has a large body with strong muscles. The mule is a sterile hybrid, but in rare cases, female mules can be fertile. Mules can form trusting relationships with their riders or trainers.

COUNT ON ME

From assisting in firefighting to transporting construction or mining materials, mules can handle the toughest tasks. In the past, about six million mules worked on farms and plantations across the United States. These numbers decreased with the introduction of machines, which replaced work animals. In many parts of South America, Asia, and Africa, mules are still used as pack animals — they can carry loads of supplies weighing up to 300 pounds.

sterile: *incapable of having offspring*
pack animals: *animals used to carry heavy loads on their backs*

Pack mules help deliver mail and supplies to remote areas.

IN THE NEWS

The University of Momboy in Venezuela started a project that uses mules to carry books into remote communities. The mules are known as *bibliomulas* (or book mules). They trek the foothills of the Andes, taking paths that even all-terrain vehicles cannot handle. As the project grows, the courier mules even help to transport laptops, movie projectors, and medicine.

Can you think of other projects that could use the help of a hardworking mule?

Quick Fact

Mules can walk up to 50 miles every day! They usually travel at about three miles per hour, maintaining a slow but steady pace.

The Expert Says...

" The mule was ready for the frontier, for war, for disaster, and for better times. ... [It] was an integral part of American life. "

— William R. Ferris, author of *Mule Trader: Ray Lum's Tales of Horses, Mules and Men*

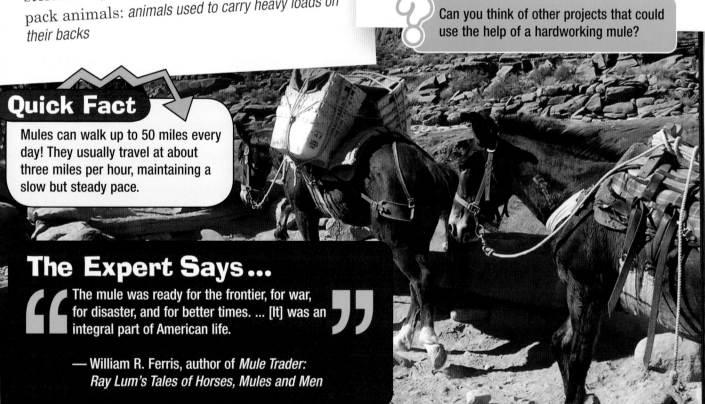

Mule vs. Donkey

Most people can tell the difference between a mule and a horse. But people often mix up mules and donkeys. Are the two really that similar? Here's a fact chart to help you sort it all out!

	MULE	DONKEY
BODY	3.5 feet tall on average	4 feet tall on average
EARS	Not quite as long as the donkey's but very sensitive to being touched	Longer than the horse's — an adaptation for cooling the body in the desert
COAT	Fine in the summer, like a horse's, but coarse in the winter, like a donkey's	Longer and coarser than a horse's coat — it helps protect the donkey from extreme heat and cold
VOICE	Combination of the horse's whinny and the donkey's bray	A raspy, brassy bray (produces an "aw-EE, aw-EE" sound)
DIET	Grass and hay	Grass and hay

Mule

Donkey

Take Note

Mules kick into #5 spot. Pack up a mule, lead it to the trail, and send it on its way. It will surely reach its destination, no matter how dangerous the situation or circumstances. In the past, mules were essential work animals in the United States. Today, they continue to help people around the world tackle tricky terrain.

• As the world continues to modernize and industrialize, what do you think will happen to working animals like the mule? Explain.

4 CAMELS

Dromedary camels are semi-domesticated animals — they graze for food on their own but respond to human commands.

CAMEL–I/SHUTTERSTOCK

CLASSIFICATION AND SIZE: Camels are mammals. They are typically about 7.5 to 11 feet long from head to tail and stand up to 7.5 feet at the shoulder.

HOW THEY HELP: Camels carry heavy loads and can perform other strenuous work; their hair and milk are very valuable.

Camels are large, strong animals that are well adapted to harsh environments and extremes of temperature. They can travel great distances across hot, dry deserts with little food or water — they can easily survive what would quickly kill most other animals. Camels also never get stuck in sand, as vehicles do, and are able to carry people and heavy loads to places that are barely reachable.

Caravans of camels have long been a common sight in the deserts of Asia and Africa. In Australia, people used camels to explore and settle in the continent beginning in the mid-1800s. Today, millions of people living in desert regions around the world still rely on camels. These tough animals help with transportation and heavy work. They are also a source of food, clothing, and even shelter.

caravans: *groups of pack animals traveling together*

CAMELS

The pad on the camel's feet supports the animal on loose sand in the same way as a snowshoe helps a person walk on snow.

PROFILE

Camels have long and curly eyelashes, which keep sand out of their eyes. Thick eyebrows protect their eyes by shielding them from the desert sun. Camels can walk easily on shifting sand because their two-toed feet have a cushion-like pad that spreads when they step on it. Most camels can go days or even weeks without food. Their humps contain stores of fat that provide energy when food is scarce. They can raise their body temperature to avoid water loss.

COUNT ON ME

Millions of people who live in desert regions in Asia and Africa depend on camels to survive. The animals pull plows, turn waterwheels to bring water to farmlands, and carry goods to markets. Camels are very important beasts of burden — they can carry loads weighing up to 1,000 pounds for 30 miles in a day! People use camel hair to make clothes, tents, and carpets. In addition, camel milk is nutritious and can be turned into different dairy products.

beasts of burden: *animals used to carry heavy loads or to perform strenuous work*

IN THE NEWS

In January 2008, the National Library of Australia put on an exhibition that paid tribute to camels and cameleers who helped open up Australia's desert interior in the 19th century. Beginning in the mid-1800s, more than 2,000 cameleers and 15,000 camels arrived from Afghanistan and what is now Pakistan. They helped build supply and communication lines across the vast Australian interior. "Cameleers assisted all major expeditions into Australia's interior," said curator Philip Jones, "and have contributed significantly to Australia's … development."

cameleers: *people who drive or ride camels*

? What is the economic importance of the camel in the dry desert areas of Asia and Africa? Do some research to explain your answer.

Quick Fact

Camels were important in desert warfare mainly due to their strength and adaptability to harsh conditions. About three million camels were used in World War I and 50,000 in World War II.

Quick Fact

Camel racing is a traditional sport in North Africa and the Middle East. Champion racing camels are worth millions of dollars. The King's Cup, held in Dubai, is possibly the sport's most important race.

The dromedary camel (left) has one hump and the Bactrian camel has two. The hump of a camel does not store water, contrary to what many people believe.

Got Milk?

Camel's milk could be the next big dairy product — it might even help solve health and hunger problems! Read these newspaper clippings to find out more.

Camel Milk: Put It on Your Face As Well As Drink It

By Pascal Fletcher, Reuters, April 3, 2007

With its hunched back, protruding teeth, facial hair, and distinctive body odor, the camel may not seem an ideal model for beauty products. Think again, says Nancy Abeiderrahmane, who runs a camel dairy in the Saharan state of Mauritania and says vitamin-rich camel milk can cleanse the body both inside and out.

By Surmounting a Few Production Humps, Camel Milk Could Bring in Billions

UN News Center, April 19, 2006

Developing camel dairy products such as milk can not only provide more food to people in arid and semi-arid areas but also give nomadic herders a rich source of income, with a $10 billion world market entirely within the realm of possibility …

nomadic: *belonging to groups that rotate between homes*

The Next Thing: Camel Milk

FAO Newsroom, April 18, 2006

Rome — In Tunisia, people will travel hundreds of [miles] to get hold of some. Herdswomen from Ethiopia and Somalia think nothing of riding a train for 12 hours to sell it in Djibouti, where prices are high. In N'Djamena, Chad, milk bars are mushrooming all over town.

Study Shows Camel's Milk Helps Children Get Over Hump of Food Allergies

By Judy Siegel-Itzkovich, *The Jerusalem Post*, December 12, 2005

Camel's milk cures severe food allergies and rehabilitates the immune system in children, according to the results of a small study in Beersheba.

rehabilitates: *restores to a condition of health*

Quick Fact

Camel's milk tastes a bit saltier than cow's milk, but it has three times the vitamin C and up to 10 times the iron content.

The Expert Says…

" Use of the camel was a great advance in the history of land transportation. Camels allowed people to establish regular contact with other groups and to establish trade routes across vast deserts. "

— Michael Woods, author of *Ancient Transportation: From Camels to Canals*

Take Note

Camels ride into the #4 spot. These tough animals were helpful to early explorers and settlers, and to troops in wartime. Today, camels continue to be of great importance to people living in harsh desert landscapes.
- What are the similarities and differences between camels and mules? Do you think camels deserve the slightly higher ranking than mules? Why or why not?

3 HORSES

Horses are powerful
animals and yet they
can also be gentle.

HORSES—ISTOCKPHOTO

CLASSIFICATION AND SIZE: Horses are mammals. They range in size from about 4.5 to 5.3 feet from the ground to the highest point of the withers (the ridge between the shoulder bones).

HOW THEY HELP: In the past, horses commonly helped people to travel and to fight wars. Today, they help out on farms and bring joy to riders of all ages.

Some people say that human history would be very different without the horse. Horses pulled the first carts and carried early nomads on their backs. Warriors have charged into battles on horseback since ancient times. People around the world have entrusted their lives to horses. No surprises there — horses are strong, intelligent, and dependable.

Today, horses are still extremely useful whether as help on the farm or as partners to mounted police. Horses that have been trained for animal-assisted therapy can offer both physical and psychological support to those in need. They can help people with disabilities strengthen their muscles and improve their range of movement. In some cases, horses can even help foster proper speech and reduce emotional difficulties.

It takes a lot of space to keep horses — stables and riding schools are often found in the rural areas. People love horses and enjoy horseback riding for recreation or sport.

foster: *promote the development of*

HORSES

PROFILE

Horses are swift and powerful animals. They are also social, and they bond with other horses in a herd or with humans. They generally sleep standing up. Horses tend to be curious. To signal what they are thinking, they use body movements such as arching their necks, showing their teeth, or widening their eyes.

COUNT ON ME

Humans have long been able to rely on horses to help make work easier and life more convenient. Today, experts believe that children with special needs and patients with certain medical conditions benefit from riding on or playing with horses. People with visual impairments sometimes rely on horses as walking guides.

IN THE NEWS

In November 2007, Patty Cooper of Waitsfield, Vermont, filed a human rights complaint against her apartment building's owners when they refused to let her keep a miniature guide horse inside her home. Cooper, who uses a wheelchair, bought her guide horse, Earl, to help her on trips to the bus stop and into town. The case has been drawing national attention. Cooper has many supporters, who think Earl should be allowed to stay. But critics argue that miniature horses are simply inappropriate service animals.

> Find out more about the benefits and drawbacks of using miniature horses as service animals. Do you think Cooper should be allowed to keep Earl in her home? Explain your answer.

Quick Fact

Literature on breeding and raising horses dates back to 1400 B.C.

Patty Cooper of Waitsfield, Vermont, with her guide horse, Earl

The Expert Says...

" For kids with disabilities, animals can also provide invaluable therapy. Riding a horse, for example, can help a child physically strengthen his or her muscles while also serving as recreation that builds self-esteem. "

— Dr. Adrian Sandler, head of the American Academy of Pediatrics' Committee on Children with Disabilities

Michael Dedrick-Dwyer (center), who has cerebral palsy and autism, takes 30-minute horse rides at a therapy center in Florida

HORSEPLAY
THAT HEALS

How can horses help patients with serious medical conditions? A type of treatment called hippotherapy relies on horses to help with physical, occupational, and speech therapy. Read these fact cards for important information.

Potential Patients

Hippotherapy can help people with the following conditions:

• Autism
• Cerebral palsy
• Down syndrome
• Learning or language disabilities
• Multiple sclerosis
• Scoliosis
• Sensory issues
• Strokes
• Traumatic brain injuries

Benefits

• A horse's walk is rhythmic and repetitive. The movement helps patients improve their balance and posture.

• A horse's movements are similar to the walking motion of a human. This helps patients who have never walked before or who have forgotten how to walk.

• The need to talk and use gestures to communicate effectively with a horse helps motivate patients, especially children, with behavioral and communication problems.

? In your opinion, what criteria should therapists consider when matching a horse to a patient? Explain your answer.

Take Note

The horse trots into the #3 spot! Horses have long been an essential helper, whether on a battlefield or a farm. They also play with us, help us travel around, transport goods for us, and help us heal. Although horses are great companions, most people do not interact with them on a daily basis. So we had to rank these great helpers below the next two animals.
• The donkey and zebra are also part of the horse family. Why do you think humans are closer to the horse? Explain.

5   4   **3**   2   1

2 CATS

It is estimated that tens of millions of cats are kept as pets around the world.

CLASSIFICATION AND SIZE: Cats are mammals. They average about eight to 10 inches tall at the shoulder.

HOW THEY HELP: Cats help us get rid of pests, warn us of dangers, and keep us company.

Imagine that your livelihood depended on the crops you grow. Now imagine that your fields are raided by mice. That could mean the end of a whole year's profit. This is when you need the help of a cat.

But there is much more to cats than just hunting and chasing pesky rodents. Their highly developed and fine-tuned senses of sight, hearing, taste, and smell make them terrific meowing alarm systems!

In ancient times, the Egyptians regarded cats as divine creatures. People convicted of killing a cat would even be put to death. Times have changed, but the popularity of cats has not. Read on to find out more about why cats take the #2 spot on our list!

CATS

PROFILE

Domestic cats spend 70 percent of the day sleeping and 15 percent of it grooming. They love to play, whether by themselves, with other cats, or with people. This keeps them mentally sharp and in shape. Cats are natural hunters — they have the instinct and abilities to survive on their own in the wild.

IN THE NEWS

In July 2007, strange news emerged about a cat called Oscar that lives at the Steere House Nursing and Rehabilitation Center in Rhode Island. Oscar has an unusual ability — he can predict when a patient is about to die. He has been correct in 25 cases. It becomes a practice for staff to call families to the nursing home when they see Oscar paying special attention to a patient.

COUNT ON ME

Some animal psychologists describe cats as selfish, solitary creatures unlikely to behave compassionately toward humans. However, although they are known as freedom-loving creatures, cats have lived alongside humans since ancient times. Cat lovers and veterinarians say that cats are great pest exterminators and everyday companions. But cats can also save lives — they have been known to smell fires, sense impending seizures, and even sniff out death!

impending: *about to occur*

The Expert Says...

"Pets can also help us by making us feel less lonely, by creating a feeling of being needed, and by encouraging social contact with others interested in animals."

— Dr. Yokoyama Akimitsu, head of the psychiatric unit, Kyosai Tachikawa Hospital, Tokyo

? Do you think you could train a cat to become a burglar alarm system? Why or why not?

Quick Fact

According to experts, cats and dogs behave differently because of motivation rather than inborn abilities. Under controlled experiments, cats can also perform highly complex tasks.

8 7 6

DEATH COMES Purring

Oscar the cat

A news article from
CBC News, July 26, 2007

A two-year-old cat has become a telltale sign of death at a Rhode Island nursing home. …

Dr. David Dosa, a geriatrician at the Steere House Nursing and Rehabilitation Center, … detailed the phenomenon Thursday in a brief essay titled "A Day in the Life of Oscar the Cat." …

"Many family members take some solace from it. They appreciate the companionship that the cat provides for their dying loved one."

Oscar was adopted as a kitten and grew up on the center's third-floor dementia unit, which treats patients with Alzheimer's, Parkinson's disease, and other illnesses.

Oscar makes his daily rounds, waiting patiently outside rooms if the doors are closed, wrote Dosa. Once inside, the gray-and-white cat jumps onto beds and appears to inspect patients by sniffing the air.

If Oscar leaves the room, the patient isn't likely to die that day, said Dosa.

---

geriatrician: *doctor who specializes in dealing with the problems and diseases of old age and aging people*
solace: *comfort; consolation*

But when the cat curls up on the bed, staff notice. They start phoning family members because the patient usually dies within four hours.

Usually indifferent and sometimes unfriendly to staff and visitors, Oscar purrs and nuzzles the patients during their final hours, Dosa said. …

Experts have speculated about Oscar's behavior, saying he could be responding to scents given off by the patient or the behavior of the nurses.

"I do think there is some biochemical reason, some odor or smell is helping the cat sense," said Dr. Joan Teno, a physician at the Steere House nursing home.

"Those behaviors have really won me over to this cat."

Quick Fact

A cat's sense of smell is 14 times as strong as that of a human.

Take Note

Cats land on the #2 spot. Their sharp senses make them an accurate and reliable source of warning in times of danger. They also provide people of all ages with companionship and comfort.
• There are millions of cat lovers in the world. What do you think is the most important reason that people like to keep cats as pets?

? What else might be able to explain Oscar the cat's ability to predict death? Think of other possible cues or signals it could be picking up on.

1 DOGS

Dogs have lived with people for more than 10,000 years — that's longer than any other animal.

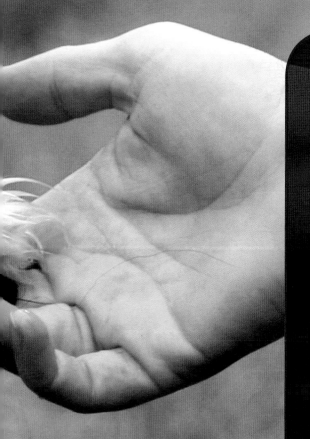

CLASSIFICATION AND SIZE: Dogs are mammals. They can be between five and 39 inches tall at the shoulder.

HOW THEY HELP: Dogs watch out for us, come to our rescue, work with us, and keep us company.

Dogs are regarded as a person's best friend. They have a habit of licking your face and bringing you things. They comfort you when you are sad, play with you when you ask, and search tirelessly until they find you.

Dogs sometimes work alongside hunters and farmers. They also help police officers and rescue workers in emergency situations. Dogs are equipped with tremendously powerful noses — their sniffing power is 44 times greater than that of humans. With training, they are able to detect anything from bombs to drugs, as well as diseases in the human body.

These canine helpers do not ask for much in return, just a simple pat on the head, a nice juicy treat, or a playful game of fetch. Whether they come from the pound or the pet shop, dogs are humans' greatest friends from the animal kingdom! They are our choice for the #1 spot.

DOGS

PROFILE

Dogs are highly sociable animals. This can account for why they are so playful, easy to train, and quick to fit into most households and social situations. Dogs are also considered to be highly intelligent and adaptable animals.

COUNT ON ME

Some dogs help people in danger; others visit with the sick and elderly to provide animal-assisted therapy. Animal psychologists say that dogs can notice emotional changes, such as when people become depressed and inactive. Studies published in 2004 and 2005 determined that dogs can also detect cancer and predict epileptic seizures. This means that dogs could one day help doctors diagnose illnesses earlier.

IN THE NEWS

In March 2007, a two-year-old golden retriever named Toby saved its owner's life by doing a canine version of the Heimlich maneuver. Toby pushed its owner, Debbie Parkhurst of Maryland, onto the floor and jumped up and down on her chest until a chunk of apple lodged in her windpipe was expelled from her airway. Toby then licked Parkhurst's face until help arrived, which kept her from passing out.

Find stories of other canine superheroes. What do all of these animals have in common?

The Expert Says...

" Certainly, there's nothing that can replace the precision of a dog's nose — and absolutely nothing that can replace a dog's heart. "

— Bob Sessions, rescue worker, U.S. Federal Emergency Management Agency

Debbie Parkhurst of Maryland with her dog, Toby

Canine Heroes of 9/11

More than 350 search-and-rescue dogs from the Federal Emergency Management Agency (FEMA) helped out with rescue efforts after the 9/11 terrorist attacks in New York City. Without these canine helpers, many of the victims trapped within the rubble that day might not have been found. Here is a collection of quotations about the heroism of the search-and-rescue dogs that worked that day:

"Some couldn't take it anymore. Rescuers asked to play fetch with Thunder. But then they'd sneak off in a corner to just be with Thunder or maybe to talk with him."

— Bob Sessions, Federal Emergency Management Agency, who works with Thunder, a rescue dog

"Not all dogs are soldiering through piles of rubble. One special unit was brought in to provide emotional support to rescue workers. They reach out to these dogs because it's OK to."

— Kitty Pilgrim, CNN correspondent

"They will search endlessly for that scent until they are called off."

— Lori Mohr, National Disaster Search Dog Foundation

"He was a great, big guy, and he was just bawling. He was crying like a baby. He couldn't talk, but he mouthed the words: 'Thank you. Thank you — and thank the dog.'"

— Louis Wardoup, volunteer, describing the reaction of a firefighter who was saved by Insee, a rescue dog

Take Note

Dogs take the #1 spot on our list of best animal helpers and friends. During happy times, they will play fetch, do some cool tricks, and keep us company. During troubled times, dogs will show us that we can truly depend on them. Their devotion to their owners is such that they will stop at nothing to ensure their safety and well-being.

• Do you agree with our #1 ranking? If you don't, why not? Explain your answer.

1

We Thought ...

Here are the criteria we used in ranking the 10 best animal helpers.

The animal:
- Is smart
- Is sociable
- Lives and associates closely with humans
- Provides emotional or physical support to people
- Works alongside people
- Has served alongside people in wars and battles
- Can be trained for specific tasks

What Do You Think?

1. Do you agree with our ranking? If you don't, try ranking these animals yourself. Justify your ranking with data from your own research and reasoning. You may refer to our criteria, or you may want to draw up your own list of criteria.

2. Here are three other animals that we considered but in the end did not include in our top 10 list: dolphins, llamas, and beavers.
   • Find out more about them. Do you think they should have made our list? Give reasons for your response.
   • Are there other animals that you think should have made our list? Explain your choices.

Index